Soul Reflections

Soul Reflections

Carroll Blair

Aveon Publishing Company

ISBN: 978-1-936430-28.4

Library of Congress Control Number
2011903864

Aveon Publishing Co.
P.O. Box 380739
Cambridge, MA 02238-0739 USA

Also by Carroll Blair

Grains of Thought
Facing the Circle
Reel to Real
Shifting Tides
Reaches
Out of Silence
Quarter Notes
By Rays of Light
Into the Inner Life
Gnosis of the Heart
Beneath and Beyond the Surface
Of Courage and Commitment
For Today and Tomorrow
In Meditation
Sightings Along the Journey
Through Desert's Fire
Offerings to Pilgrims
Human Natures
(Of Animal and Spiritual)
Atoms from the Suns of Solitude
Colors of Devotion
Voicings
Through the Shadows
As the World Winds Flow

What is worth spending
your life on . . . in . . .
with . . .? That which
death cannot defeat.

2.

The true essence of a human life,
its calling and guiding principle
begins its realization at the
dawn of spiritual awakening.

3.

The source of your being, and
from where you have come . . .
what the spiritual energy of your
life is ever working to draw
your attention to or remind you of.

4.

You are part of all creation.
How then can you not share
in all of creation?

5.

The divine offers to humankind
so much more than the earth
on which it stands.

6.

The eternal is an endless font
of creative power, and to the degree
that one has joined to the eternal,
one may partake of that power.

7.

To move further into light
is to move further into freedom.

8.

In the physical all are powerless
beings able to be annihilated
at any moment, vulnerable to the
perils of life. In the spiritual
nothing of the world, not all its
armies combined can destroy
its power, can extinguish its light.

9.

The pathway to the eternal
is always open, but like
any other pathway, it will
not go to you — it is you
who must go to it.

10.

Life has infinite frontiers to
be discovered, not limited by
the world of matter.

11.

When you realize that
what you are able to see is
not all there is to be seen,
you begin to see more.

12.

It is wonder that leads one
to gift after gift, to treasure
after treasure.

13.

One need not know the nature of
the Source, or why it is, or where
it is from . . . one only needs to
feel it for it to enrapture the soul.

14.

First the mind opens, then
the heart, releasing the power
of spirit drawing from the
origin from which one came,
of which one is part.

15.

The Source is within you, and
you will never recognize it
anywhere else before
finding it inside yourself.

16.

The eternal is not somewhere
other — it is here, has
always been here, waiting
for your arrival.

17.

Removing veils, dissolving
barriers, clearing away the false
replacing it with harvests
of truths nourished by the
sun of Truth . . . the journey
from darkness to light.

18.

To grow spiritually is to
grow closer to some things
and away from others.

19.

The highest path is that
which leads to where neither
age nor time matters.

20.

Wanderings of the temporal
take one everywhere
but anywhere.

21.

The shortest distance of the
spiritual journey takes one
further than the longest
of earthly journeys.

22.

Every moment is a transport
of coming and going, inviting
to move one toward the
next awakening.

23.

One wakens to the beginnings of
wisdom only when one knows
that he has been sleeping.

24.

The awareness of enlightenment
is mindfulness, heartfulness,
soulfulness.

25.

Before transcendence there
must be transformation.

26.

To open one's being is to
expand it, to deepen it, to set it
on a course of evolution.

27.

Of the places most worth
venturing to, the body
cannot take you.

28.

The spiritual journey is not
a venture of gather and gain
but of shedding, of leaving
behind, of letting go.

29.

The spirit knows nothing of "I."

30.

No treasure of the eternal
reveals itself to ego.

31.

To bound from the ledge of ego
is not to fall, but to rise.

32.

With every softening of heart
and deepening of mind new
light and energy are released,
and spiritual truth that much
closer to being discovered.

33.

To see with increasing
clarity one must continually
bring one's life to a place
it has never been.

34.

The spirit is whole, yet its
journey is never complete.

35.

The last motion of each
stage of enlightenment
births one into the next.

36.

Discipline holds the key to
the part of life which is its
kingdom . . . (i.e., the spiritual).

37.

A seed is not realized
until it begins to grow.

38.

Life is forever challenging one
to come to greater life, and
helps those along who
take up the challenge.

39.

The freedom *from* comes first,
followed by the freedom to . . .

40.

The greater joy does not come from
having more today than you did
yesterday, but needing less.

41.

Higher than being committed to
spiritual development is being
committed to what it represents.

42.

The best offerings of the
everyday world do not equal
the blessings of the lowest stage
of spiritual development.

43.

Life's energies are sacred,
yet how often have they
been squandered on endeavors
that are unworthy of them.

44.

The wonders of the eternal
cannot be recognized or
appreciated in the shallows
of ego-thought.

45.

Ego thrives in the man-made
swamps of delusion; in the
ocean of spirituality it is lost.

46.

In the natural world the sail
pays no charge for the wind;
not so, in the spiritual.

47.

The transcendent takes one as far
as one has the courage to go.

48.

How different is the nature of life
to one whose interests lie with
the eternal from one who has
stationed his life in the temporal.

49.

Every growth brings its
own obstacles that must be
overcome before the attainment
of higher growth.

50.

In the spiritual realm
drawing nearer means going
further; drawing higher
means going deeper.

51.

One's higher self must be
created, for one's higher self
is synonymous with one's
deeper self, which
must be created.

52.

As the infant hasn't the
expressions of the adult it
will become, so spiritual
development in its infancy
hasn't the expressions of
what it could one day become.

53.

Each life begins as the
opening to a horizon . . .
whether it continues to open
and how much it opens depends
on the one to whom the
life has been given.

54.

Almost everything in the
everyday world can wait.
What of the spiritual
should wait . . .

55.

What is to be learned
that is more important
than what is, and what
is not important?

56.

A life that is filled with
trivial endeavor may feel
full, but never fulfilled.

57.

The measure of a life is the sum
of its preoccupations.

58.

The miracle of human life
is its ability to aspire
to higher life amid the
banalities and brutalities
of the world.

59.

One who pursues growth
rather than happiness realizes
the strongest happiness.

60.

The capacity to grow is
itself a wondrous gift.

61.

The spiritual path is the highest
path, but also the most humble.

62.

They who wish to behold and not
possess or control understand
the essence of the principal journey.

63.

Enlightenment is not something
that is fixed but ever growing,
expanding into new regions
of wisdom and light.

64.

With the increase of mind, of
heart, of spirit and the gifts they
manifest comes an increase
of responsibility to life.

65.

Only animal nature is
solely interested in
taking and receiving.

66.

One doesn't achieve a better
life by acquiring more
"things," but by becoming
a better human being.

67.

Greed, avarice, selfishness
are as dams blocking the
tributaries of love, yearning
to reach the lives of all.

68.

When ego is speaking
nothing of the spiritual is
listening . . . (or speaking).

69.

The power of ego to that of
selflessness is as a candle
to the power of the sun.

70.

The goal of achieving in
spiritual endeavor is to learn
how to serve life well.

71.

It is always time to love.

72.

One lives in the humanity
of one's life to the degree
that one contributes
to life's positives.

73.

When giving of oneself
to life one is not concerned
or preoccupied with what
life is giving in return.

74.

One feels only so much
as one is brave enough
to feel.

75.

To be a healing force in
the world one must allow
one's heart to break.

76.

A life of giving, no matter its
measure will ever be more
than the life that is primarily
focused on receiving.

77.

There is nobility in all kindness,
and kindness in all nobility.

78.

If you do not help, console, attend
to those in need who cross your path
to the best of your ability,
are you on the right path . . .

79.

Love is born in the heart,
but grows beyond it.

80.

If one does not say yes
to love, one's "yes" to
everything else is as
good as no.

81.

No fruit comes forth
from the ground that is
hard and cold.

82.

One cannot see love but
through the eyes of love, feel
love but through the heart
of love, give love but
through the spirit of love.

83.

The way of the spiritual
can turn sorrow to joy,
enmity to compassion,
and selfish thought to
selfless action.

84.

In every moment there is
something waiting to be
learned . . . something
waiting to be done.

85.

Example is the lesson
that is always genuine.

86.

No one who has mined the
spiritual is without yearning
to share the treasure that
has been discovered.

87.

Life is always ready to
accommodate new offerings
to be laid upon its table.

88.

All are invited to partake
of the bountiful gifts of life,
but also invited to add
something to it.

89.

By the very act of
cultivating an affinity
for the best of humanity
one adds to its best.

90.

There is more darkness in the
human world than there is light,
but does one have a right to
complain about it if one doesn't
bring to the world some light . . .

91.

Though a kindness
may go unnoticed it is
never done in vain.

92.

Humans have an excuse
when their body one day
fails them; not so, when
they fail their spirit.

93.

It is more important where one
has been inside oneself than
outside, spiritually speaking.

94.

The primary work of a human
being is the inner work, which
leads the way to the spiritual.

95.

One is not only responsible
for the actions of one's life,
but also the inactions
in one's life.

96.

The longer the inner work
is avoided the harder
it is to begin.

97.

One must create the soil
from which the harvests of
one's life may flourish.

98.

The state of one's mind, one's
heart, one's spirit is the state
of one's true wealth.

99.

Riches are not only in what
one has, but in what one hasn't —
(i.e., in what one is free of).

100.

They deny themselves more
than life denies them who go
the way of the trivial.

101.

Many fear the relinquishing
of ego because they fear
they'll be lost without it, not
realizing how lost they are
by holding on to it.

102.

The more one adheres to ego the
more dying there is, the less
living in one's life.

103.

The spirit cannot fully wake
until the ego fully dies.

104.

What is "personality" but the
abode of ego barring the
way to purification, to
enlightenment, to transcendence.

105.

One's spirit is always free
from the bindings of the
material world, but some
do not know it (or
choose not to know it).

106.

The temporal exists on
borrowed time, invested by the
wise in the eternal.

107.

The world of the fleeting is a grand
illusion keeping all who are drawn
to it away from truth, from light,
from the true treasures of
life, and of their lives.

108.

To spend life in the pursuit
of things that are as good as
nothing . . . is this not to
live, for nothing?

109.

Everyday life is filled
with shadow impressions
seriously taken by many
for substance.

110.

Veritable love, truth, wisdom
exists uncorrupted, ageless and
profound in the eternal.
In the temporal there is only
mirage, stand-ins, substitutes
for the genuine article.

111.

To care not for the false
of the world in all its deceptions
is to let nothing of the false
power over you.

112.

Many concern themselves with
being shortchanged in mundane
affairs, unaware of how much
they shortchange themselves
in matters of the spiritual.

113.

It is grave folly to live one's life
trying to hold on to what will be
destroyed and not embrace the
dimension of one's life that
can never be destroyed.

114.

How can spiritual treasure be
revealed to those who live their
lives with greater interest in the
feasts of the material than in
the feast of the soul . . .

115.

There is a price to pay for
every step toward the light,
and a price to pay for every
step away from it.

116.

The spiritual path is about
clearing space, each step
needing to be cleared
before it is taken.

117.

Nothing that is let go of from the
temporal doesn't present an opportunity
to replace it with something
far more valuable.

118.

To know the greatest
experiences that life has to
offer, one must be willing
to venture into the unknown.

119.

Spiritual awakening is first,
bewildering; second, arresting;
third, transforming;
fourth, a rising.

120.

As there are corporal places
that can be reached by a number
of roads, and others by only
one, so there are stations of
the spirit that can be reached a
number of ways, and others
by only one.

121.

The trail to the divine never
turns cold — only the courage
and commitment of those
who give up the search.

122.

Paradise is entered from
within, but the journey
must still be made
in order for one to enter.

123.

There is no limit for the
spirit to love, to sublimate, to
grow . . . only a limit of
humankind's willingness to
open to all it has to give.

124.

The major blessing in life
is not in what life gives,
but in the opportunity
to earn what is given.

125.

Sometimes to add something
to one's life is to create a
minus; sometimes to subtract
something is to create a plus.

126.

Without discipline all is lost.

127.

The way to the eternal
demands everything, but also
holds the highest gifts
that can be received.

128.

To the measure that ego
is present the inner journey
has not been taken.

129.

To get further away from one's
"I" (one's ego) one must go
deeper into oneself.

130.

Spiritual ground is not attained
by moving upward outside,
but moving deeper inside.

131.

As ego diminishes true power
begins to grow, the illusion of
power then fading to shadow.

132.

What is real is for always,
lined with eternal light.

133.

Nothing of the spiritual
allows one to approach
with pride.

134.

The spiritual dimension cares not
for what man wants, yet gives those
more than they can ever want,
can ever dream of who go to it
willing to work, willing to
pay the price for its treasure.

135.

The spiritual provides one the
means by which it is paid for —
that must also be earned.

136.

The value of a journey is
always (objectively speaking)
in what it has produced.

137.

One who moves through life
accompanied by love, truth,
magnanimity and direction of
noble purpose cannot be kept
from the primary human goal
of self-realization in the higher
form, which opens all pathways
to wisdom and enlightenment.

138.

Every day is a test of one's
fortitude and sincerity.

139.

Does not the earth bring
forth with constant resolution,
and does not the dutiful spirit
endeavor to do the same . . .

140.

True freedom is not the
freedom to always do what
one wants, but to do
what one must.

141.

Without inner work that develops a
maturity and awareness capable of
serving the spiritual dimension, one
could labor day after day from dawn
to dusk in the outer world doing
whatever for the whole of one's life,
and it would bear no meaning.

142.

One who can appreciate only
what can be touched by the hand
has not the power of spirit
to touch the eternal.

143.

To go as far as one can
go requires that one be
connected to what is always.

144.

Eternal life is not something to be
waited to experience after death,
but to be experienced now in the
life that one is living.

145.

Courage is the fuel that
drives the spirit.

146.

The sun projects light, but if one
were far enough away it could not
be received . . . (the same
with spiritual light).

147.

In the realm of the eternal
nothing of a corrupted
nature can exist.

148.

To not feel content with the
goings-on of the day-to-day
world is a blessing, the feeling
telling you there is more, and
that you are more, than this.

149.

Some wish just to get through
the day; others wish to savor it,
to dance with it; to give love
and thankfulness to it.

150.

The day-to-day world
is the master cage
of the human world.

151.

Their lives are most
confined whose lives are
not conducted from within.

152.

The butterfly in the net
is no longer a butterfly.

153.

The least free are they who
have yet to assume the
spiritual responsibility
of their lives.

154.

A life is only as rich, as deep,
as real as what it has
pursued and embraced.

155.

What is real? That which
nothing can destroy.

156.

The world of earthly ambition
is an ego-driven world, a
frivolous world, antithetical
to the goals of the spiritual.

157.

To not find one's way to the
eternal is to live one's days
in darkness, moving from
nowhere to nowhere.

158.

Even the dimmest of light
will cause pain to one who
has long been in the dark.

159.

The eyes of the heart, the
mind, the soul are created by
the wound of awakening.

160.

How many are satisfied with a
reference to the divine in place of a
union with its substance, for this would
force them to open, compel them to grow,
to create soil for the spiritual seed lying
dormant inside them, to face the light,
then move into light, to be born anew
and again, anew, braving whatever pains
of spiritual birth that must be borne,
to then be ready to engage, to embrace,
to give to the divine, no longer to fear it
or admire it only from afar, the distance
long protecting them from the demands of
its power, but also keeping them from the
realization of what human life can be.

161.

All that brings pain to the
soul comes on the wings
of instruction.

162.

If not for pain the
shield of illusion would
never be broken.

163.

As a beautiful rainbow paints
a sunlit sky after a storm,
so does beauty and peace
brighten the soul after a
period of spiritual struggle.

164.

The spiritual quest is a
series of discoveries revealing
itself . . . revealing oneself.

165.

When one comes to a place one
finds impossible to get beyond
it is because there is something
one needs to learn or do there,
preventing one from moving on
until it is done.

166.

Sometimes it is fortune,
not misfortune that places
the obstacle before you.

167.

The more enlightened, the
more the answers are sought
from within . . . (need to be
sought from within).

168.

The light is within you, either
veiled or shining through.

169.

You are born with the
eternal presence of your life,
but it is you who must
make its discovery.

170.

One could know everything
of the material world there is to
know and not experience the depths
of greater wonder by going
the way of the spiritual.

171.

There is always something
more, somewhere further to go
in the spiritual quest.

172.

Human achievement is only a
fraction of what could be achieved
if brave enough, selfless enough,
humble enough.

173.

Forces of the body do not
strengthen without effort,
and so it is with those
of mind and spirit.

174.

It is not wisdom if it
does not lead to greater
wisdom; not love
if it does not lead
to greater love.

175.

When humanity doesn't strive
to aspire and overcome
it undermines its very
reason for being.

176.

The door to human progress
is closed by complacency.

177.

Perseverance itself is a
courage and a strength.

178.

The more one tries to make
life easier for himself the harder
it is to find his way to the
better part of himself.

179.

They speak falsely who
proclaim that the way
to anywhere that is
somewhere is easy.

180.

If you are able to stand long
contented on a goal completed,
was it a goal worth achieving?

181.

One who feels that he has
"arrived" in the spiritual sense
has yet to begin *the journey*.

182.

The probing spirit is always
on the way to a breakthrough
to release a creative current
on the other side — then on
to another breakthrough.

183.

There are things the human
spirit can do that the great
forces of Nature cannot do.

184.

To transform, to transcend, to
direct that transcendence . . .

185.

What one is capable of
becoming is ever to
be learned.

186.

So many use their life to pursue
earthly fortunes, not realizing that
their life itself is a fortune — the
greatest fortune of all when guided
by the consciousness that is
aware of its value.

187.

Time is everywhere at once
giving everyone in every moment
the same amount, but how diverse
the things it is spent on, and the
measures of wisdom or folly
behind its employment.

188.

Often has a love for life
been mistaken for a love
for its pageantry.

189.

If there is one thought
that should be etched for
a lifetime upon the mind
it is that all of earthly
existence is fleeting.

190.

Everyone is running out of time;
while this is happening those in union
with the eternal have the gift of
timelessness flowing out of them.

191.

Existence is experienced by all,
death is experienced by all, but
life is not experienced by all.

192.

The degeneration of flesh is
not as woeful a phenomenon
as a degeneration of spirit.

193.

Many want the finest
wines, the richest cuisines,
but have no appetite for
spiritual sustenance.

194.

Everything that stands in
the way between one and the
divine is self-generated,
coming from within.

195.

Where there is not profound
gratitude, profound tenderness,
profound awe of the majesty
of life, enlightenment
cannot be present.

196.

One moment of enlightenment
is worth more than a lifetime
of day-to-day consciousness.

197.

To know the depth of a
human being is to know
the inner work that
has been done.

198.

A greater gift cannot be given to
those around one than an honored
commitment to the inner work.

199.

No day passes without another
opportunity to grow.

200.

The major obstacle to growth
is excuses for not growing.

201.

If the aim of life were
to avoid pain, nothing
would ever be born.

202.

Life could no more exist
without suffering than
suffering could exist
without life.

203.

The good physician works to learn
all that can be learned from a fever
before it breaks. The spirit-venturer
true in his or her seeking works to
learn all they can from a fever of
suffering before it breaks.

204.

How often is something
thought to manifest only
sorrow when beneath it
lies an abundance of joy.

205.

Where there is deep love
the highest possibilities
are most accessible.

206.

To seek not the illusion
of security from the temporal,
but the deathless embrace
of the eternal . . .

207.

A giving of one's life to the
unchanging, then looking out
into the world to see what
might be done to make
a better change . . .

208.

As you are to the world
so shall your spirit be to you.

209.

One *lives* so long as one loves.

210.

The spirit also has its morning
sun where everything warms
and glows in its radiance.

211.

In the absence of selflessness
one cannot be close to living a
life rich in beauty and wonder.

212.

All lives are temporal,
but the noble life is the
one that reveres and protects
the sanctity of the eternal.

213.

To be spiritually inspired
is to be forever astonished
by the great miracle of life.

214.

What is the happiness worth that is
not accompanied by the sublime?

215.

It is the journey that leads one to
higher love, wisdom and truth that
brings one to higher purpose.

216.

The spiritual too needs its warriors.

217.

Believe there is an eternal law
that if you dare to seek and
persevere, you will find.

218.

Beyond manhood or womanhood
into spirithood . . . into the mines
of treasure lighting within.

219.

Defeat the ego and win
not the treasure of a lifetime,
but of an eternity.

220.

They who have lived with light,
by light, for light have no fear
of a final darkness.

221.

To the enlightened spirit every
day is a day of thanksgiving.

222.

What else matters
but the business of
loving and creating?

223.

To be set free is to
be taken hold of
in the spiritual.

224.

Spiritual love is demanding,
yet also serves, also honors.

225.

It is the spirit that breathes
meaning into human life.

.

226.

To let go of the day-to-day
world is to take in the
whole of the world.

227.

One can almost hear the whisper
of the temporal saying to those
who make it their home: "Why
are you here? There is little
I can give to you, nothing of true
value . . . in my domain your
energies evaporate like a morning
mist, leaving you (what) for
all your efforts? Why do you not
turn to the eternal where
blessing beyond measure
is waiting for you . . . "

228.

The highest things are
above all forms of "I,"
born of and belonging
to the glorious mystery
of the divine.

229.

If not for the mystery what
reason to live would there be?

230.

Life will constantly astound
you, if you allow it to.

231.

Transcend the animal of
human-being, and behold the
world that opens to you.

232.

How can true life be
attained until it is lived
through the eternal . . .

233.

Turn from what is
false and feel the rising
of truth within you.

234.

Life is forever coming to life
to those whose lives are
filled with light.

235.

A servant of the spiritual will
always be more than any king
of earthly design.

236.

To get to the rapture that
draws its breath from the light . . .

237.

You are offered a kingdom of
unimagined wealth, here, in this
life — a wealth that, once
discovered instills a passion of
yearning to ever be giving it
away — a wealth as inexhaustible
as the yearning to give; that
of the spirit, realized in the heart,
flowing out in a stream of
everlasting love.

Like the sun shining above
crowning the earth, let the
sun of your spirit be the
crown of your life.

ABOUT THE AUTHOR

Carroll Blair is an author of more than twenty books and the recipient of numerous awards. His work has been well endorsed and commendably reviewed. Among his titles cited for distinction are *Through the Shadows*, winner of the Pacific Book Awards, and *Quarter Notes*, winner of the Sharp Writ Book Awards. He is an alumnus of the Boston Conservatory and lives in Massachusetts.

www.ingramcontent.com/pod-product-compliance
Lightning Source LLC
Chambersburg PA
CBHW020040040426
42331CB00030B/106